VOTE 2012 Presidential Election Coloring Book

OBAMA
Perry
CAIN
PAUL
Bachmann
Romney
Santorum
Gingrich

OFFICIAL COLORING BOOK • COLOR, COLOR, COLOR •

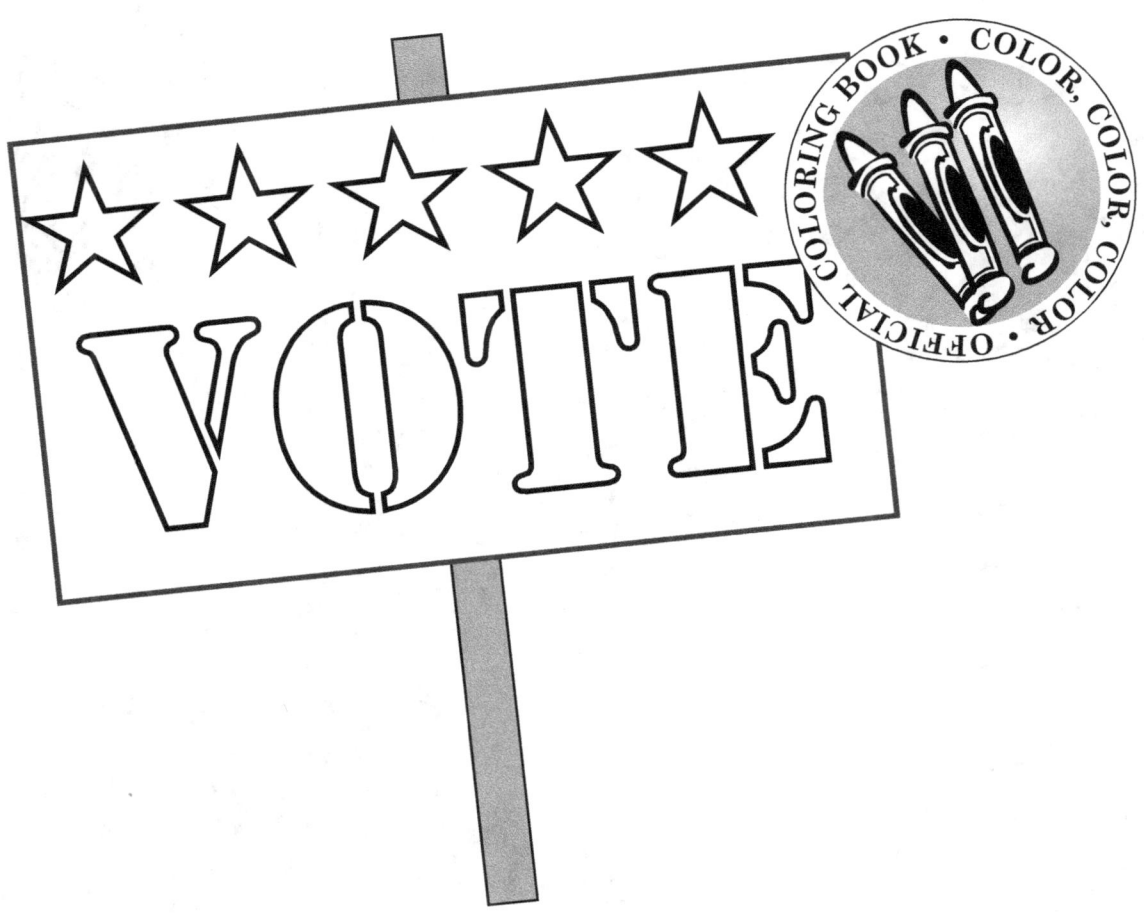

Vote 2012 Coloring Book by J. Bruce Jones

© Copyright J. Bruce Jones 2011 All rights reserved.

Original map illustrations by J. Bruce Jones and the World of Maps Collections

Some images in this book are from and under copyright of www.graphicsfactory.com, © GraphicsFactory.com and www.novadevelopment.com, © Nova Development Corporation • All rights reserved

J. Bruce Jones
661 Washington Street
Norwood, MA 02062
781-255-7171 • bruce@bjdesign.com
www.brucejonespublishing.com

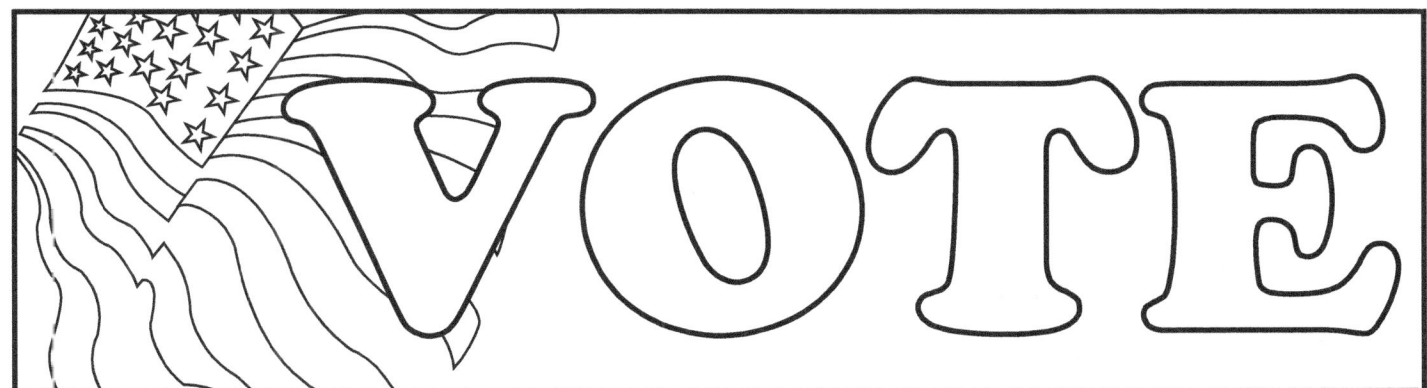

Voting Bumper Stickers

"Before he enter on the Execution of his Office, he shall take the following Oath or Affirmation:"

Article Two, Section One, Clause Eight of the United States Constitution

"I do solemnly swear (or affirm) that I will faithfully execute the Office of President of the United States, and will to the best of my Ability, preserve, protect and defend the Constitution of the United States."

Lincoln Memorial

President Thomas Jefferson

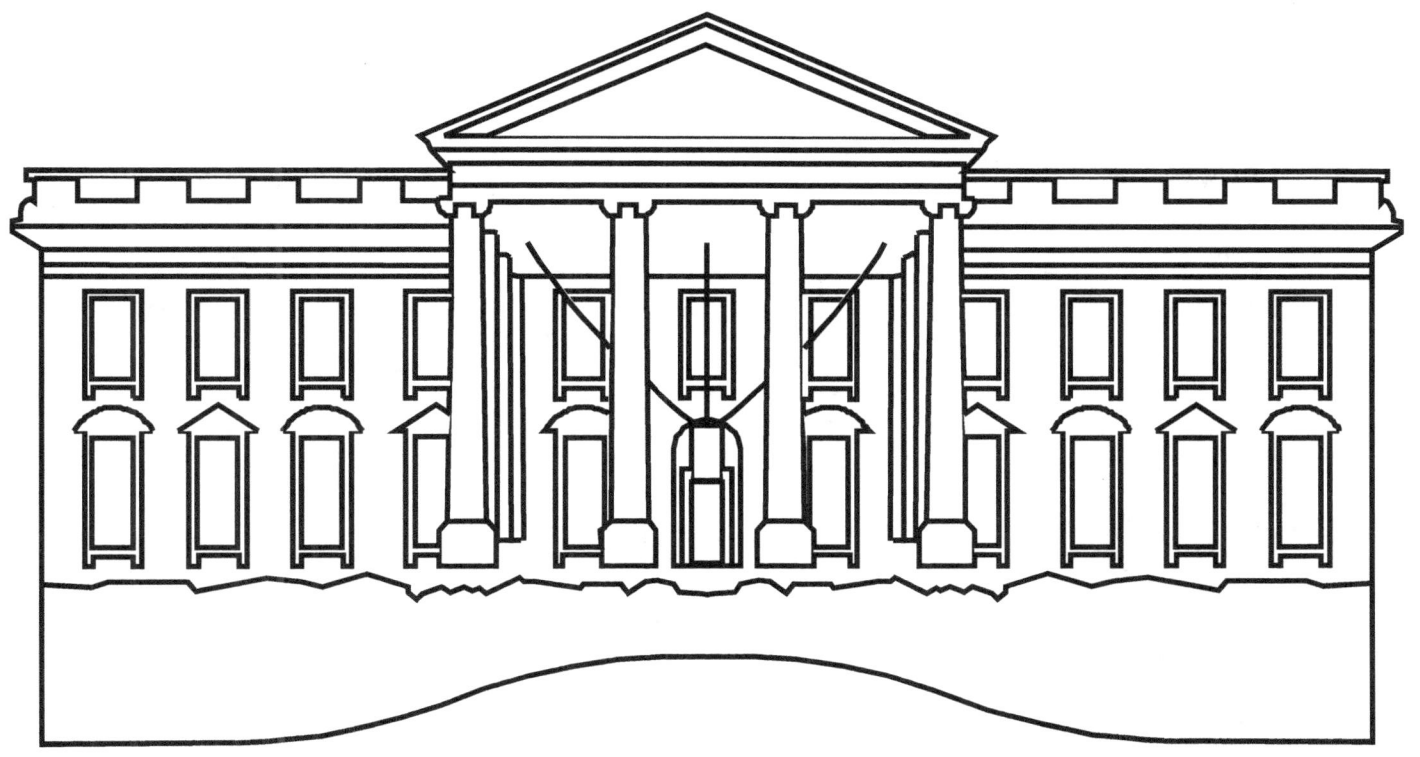

The White House

Independence Hall
Philadelphia, PA

Voting Buttons

Make Your Own Voting Buttons

UNITED STATES of AMERICA

President Barack Obama

US Supreme
Court Building

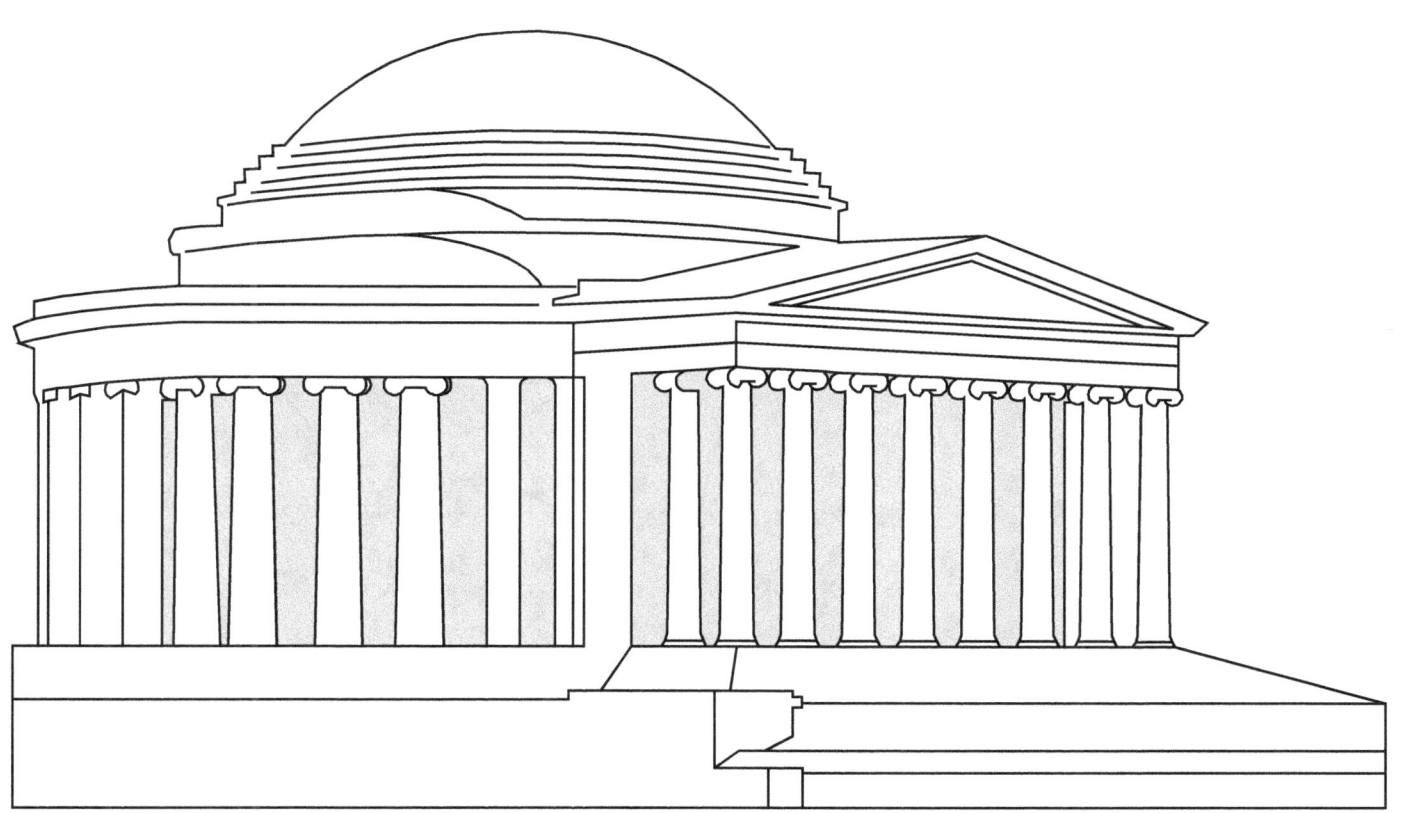

Jefferson Memorial

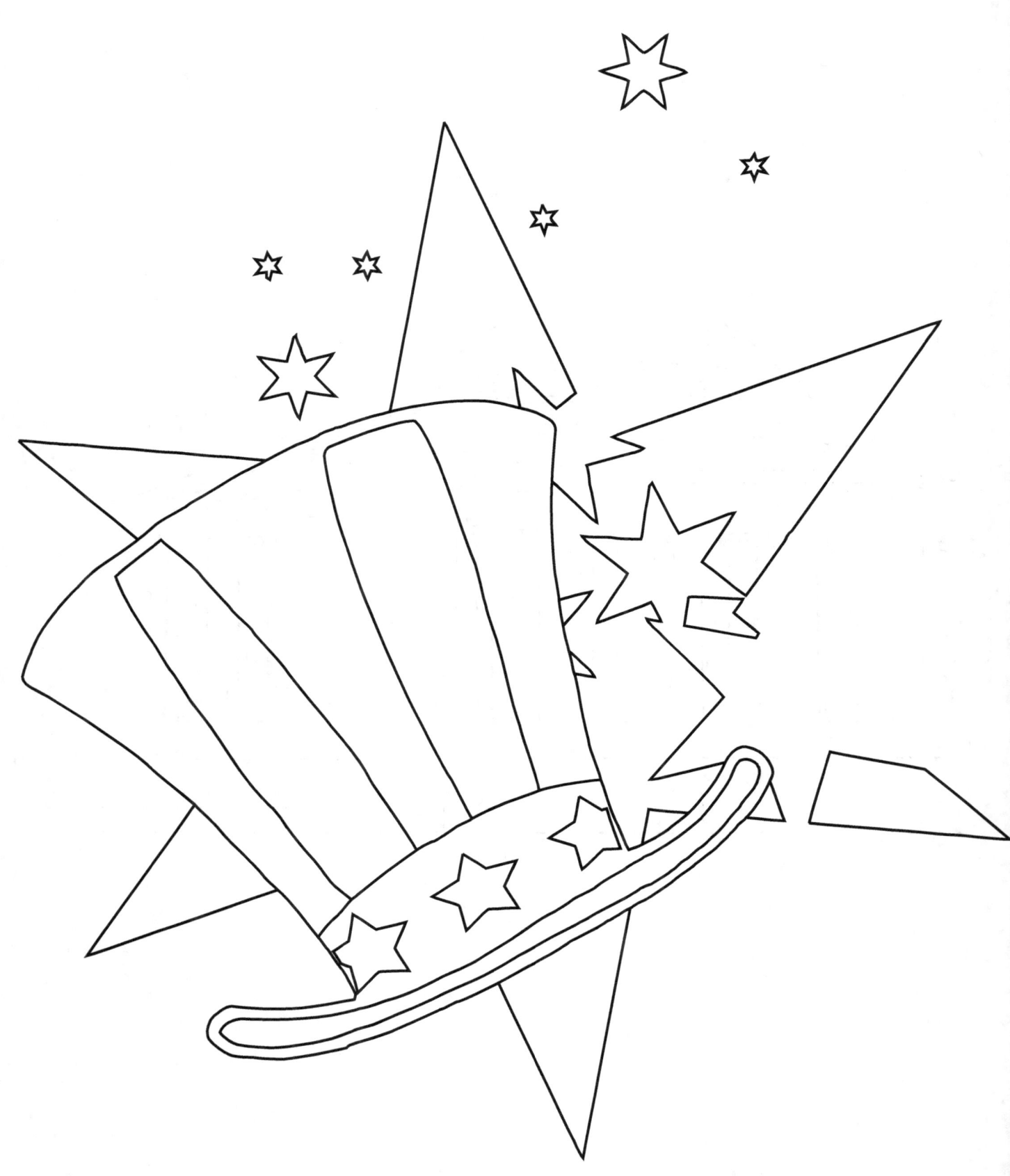

Former Governor
Mitt Romney

Democratic Party ✶

U.S. Rep. Ron Paul

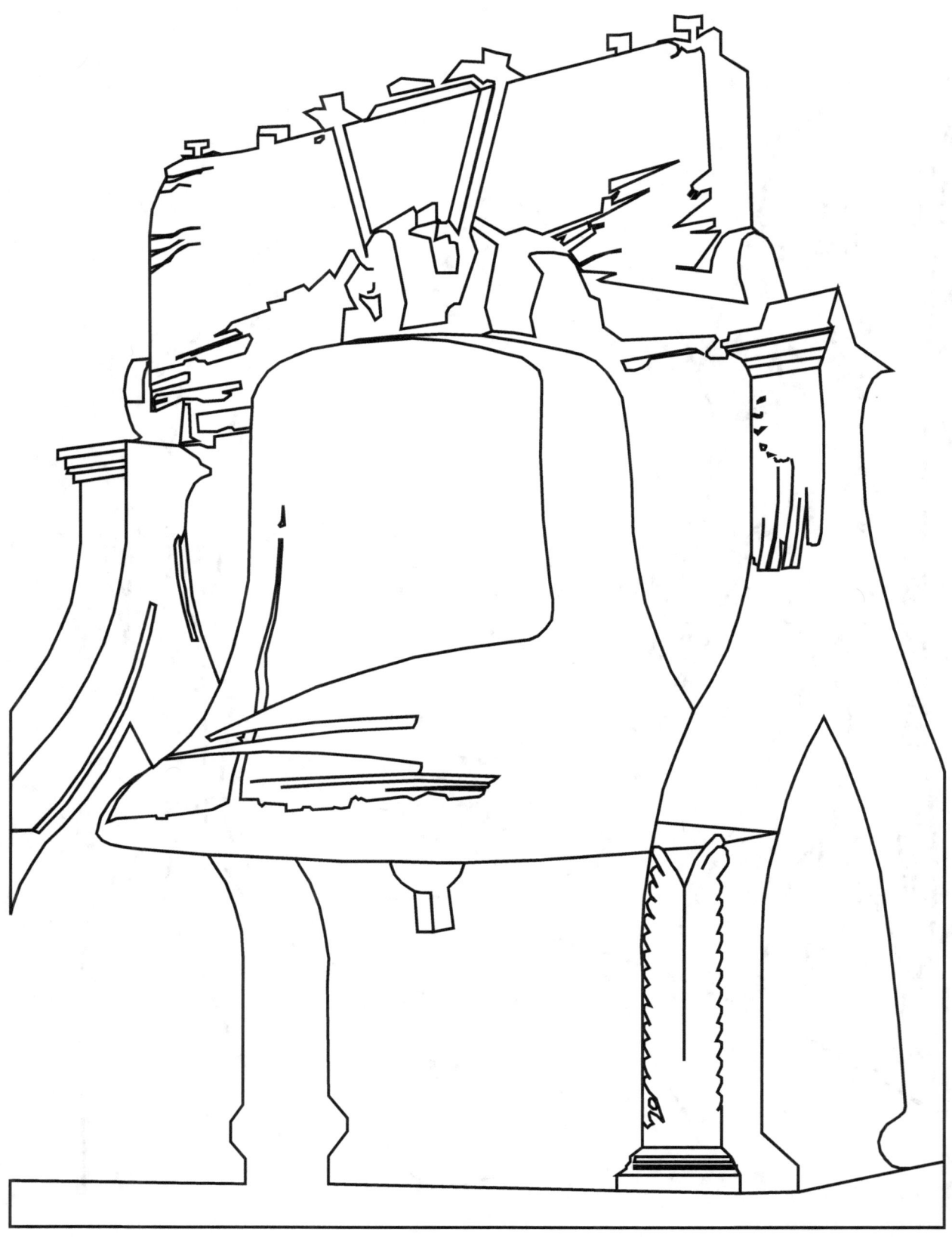

Liberty Bell

Statute of Liberty

Former Ambassador
Jon Huntsman

Former Speaker of the House
Newt Gingrich

Republican Party

Commercial use of the Presidential Seal is
prohibited by United States Code, so we made
up our own fun seal to color.

US Capital Building

UNITED STATES

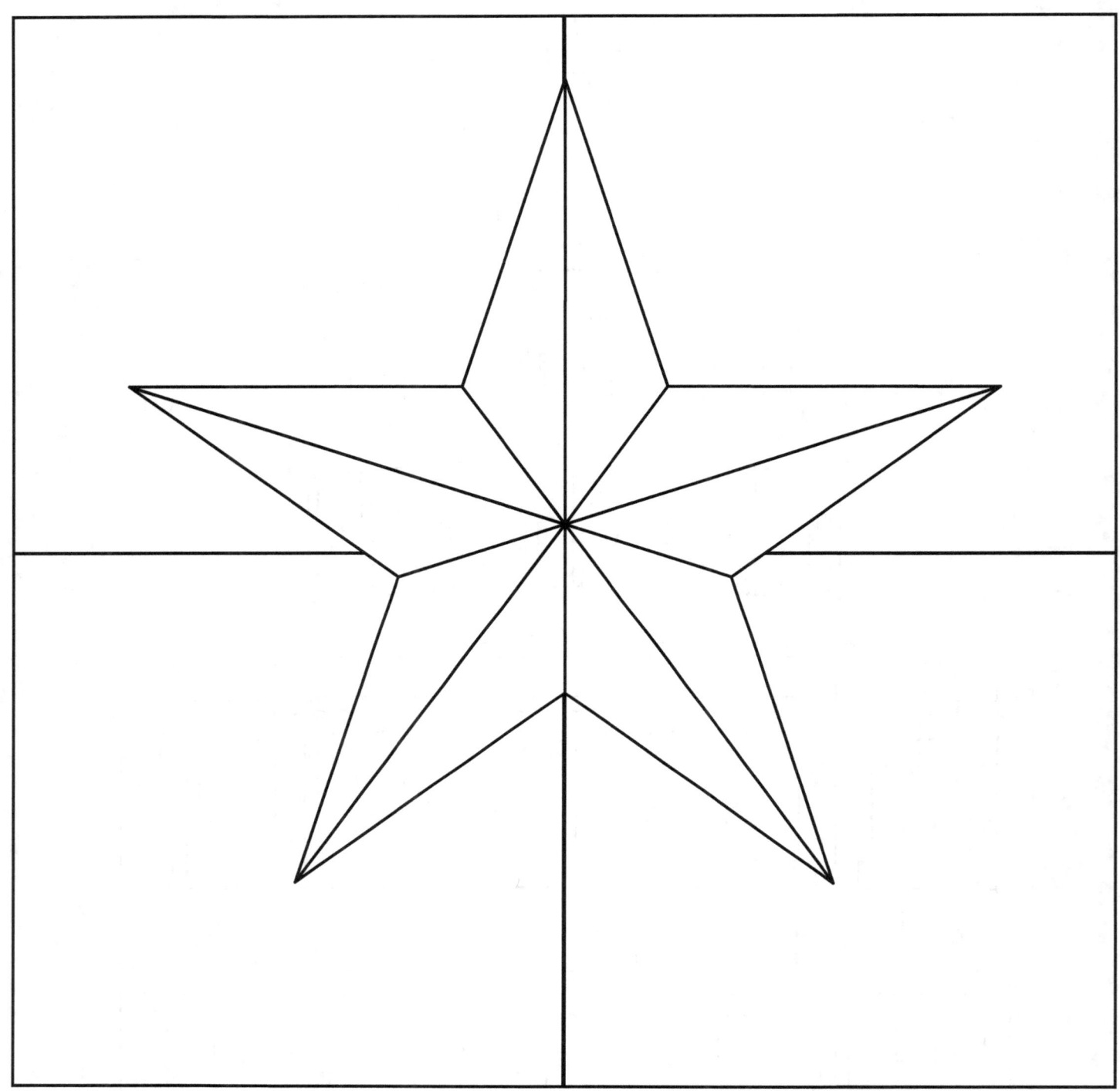

# of AMERICA

Uncle Sam

Herman Cain

⋆ VOTE 2012 Presidential Election Coloring Book ⋆

United States of America

President Abraham Lincoln

Former U.S. Senator
Rick Santorum

Statute of Liberty

U.S. Rep Michele Bachmann

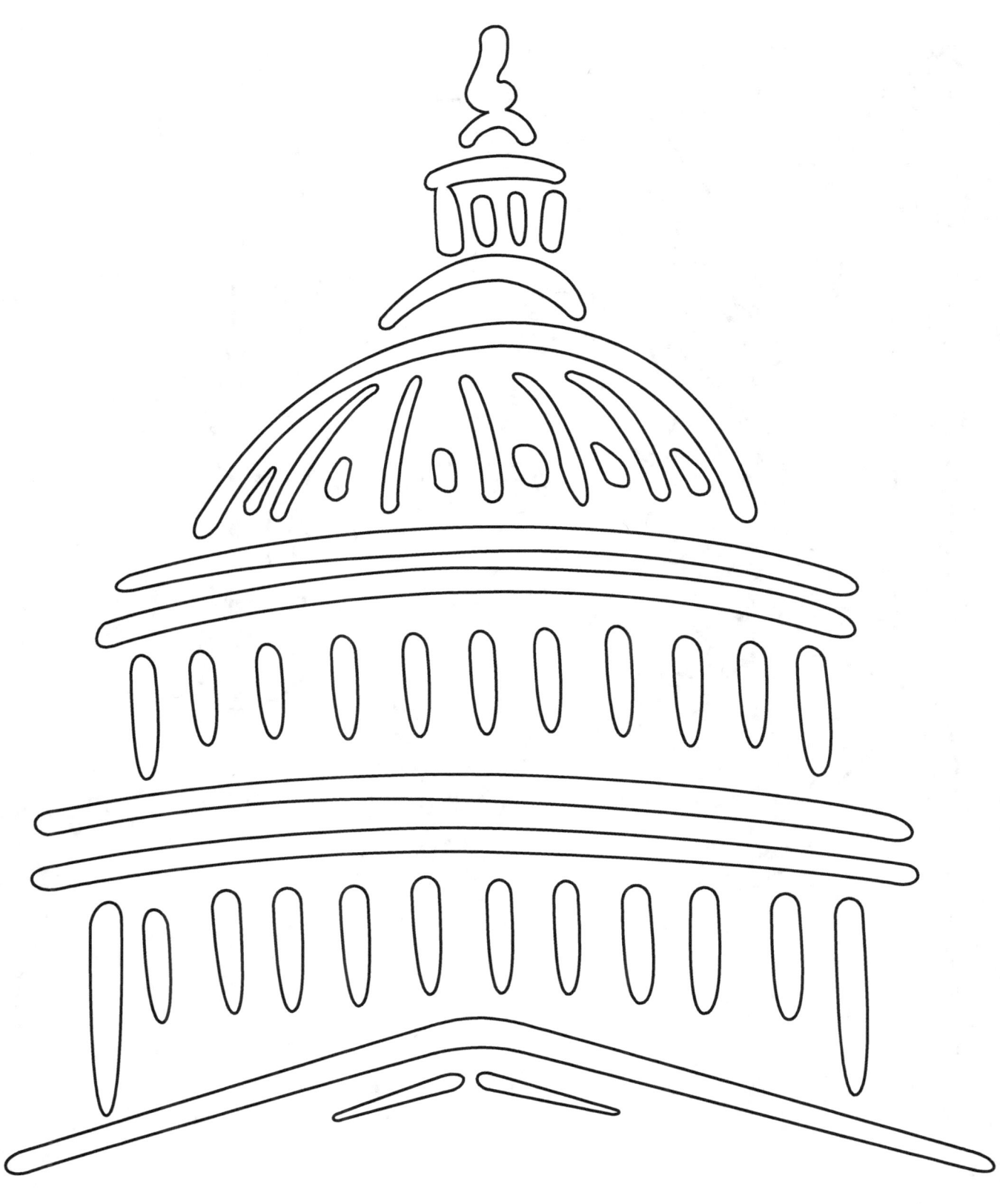

Capital Dome

The White House

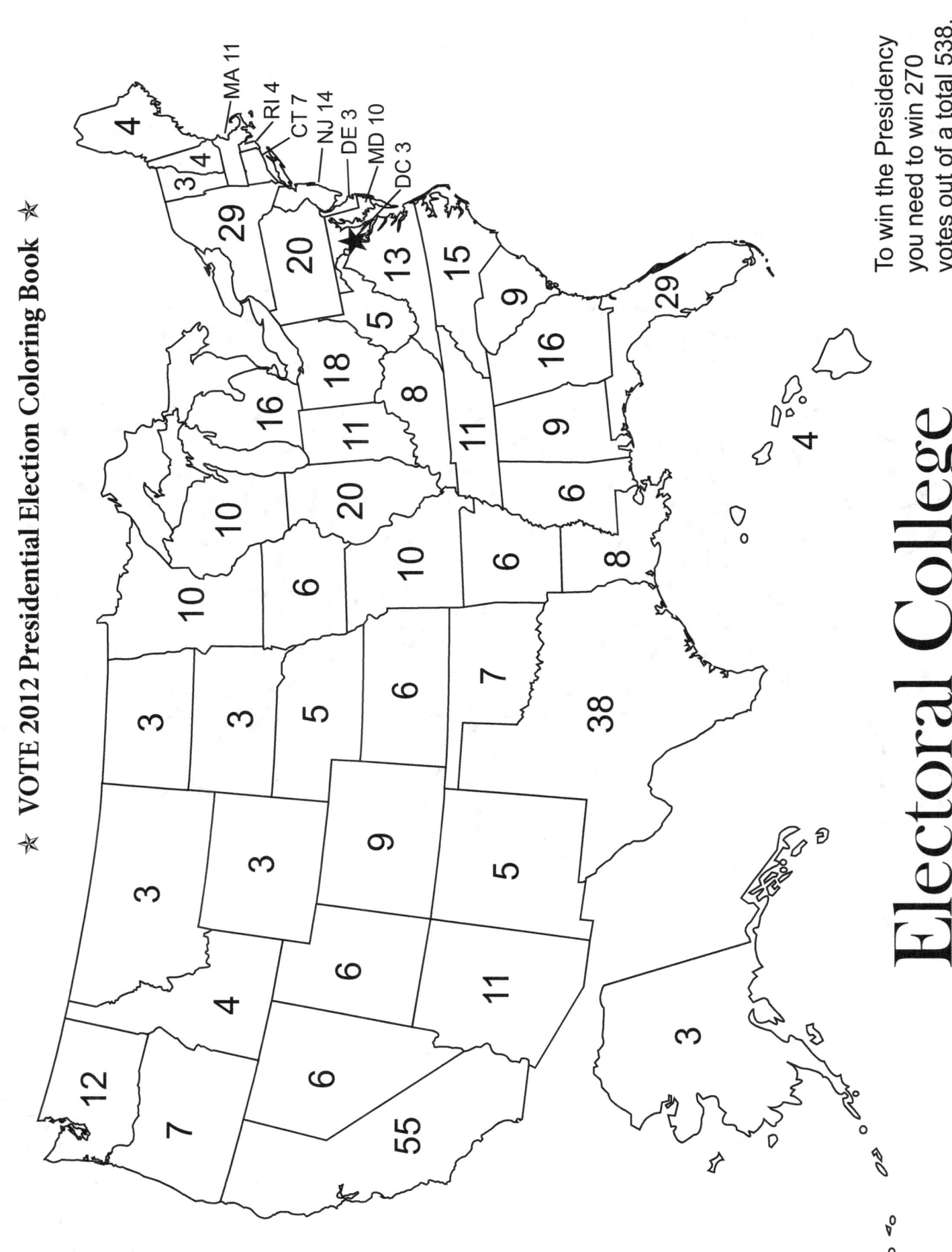

MA 11
RI 4
CT 7
NJ 14
DE 3
MD 10
DC 3

Electoral College

To win the Presidency
you need to win 270
votes out of a total 538.

Governor Rick Perry

President George Washington

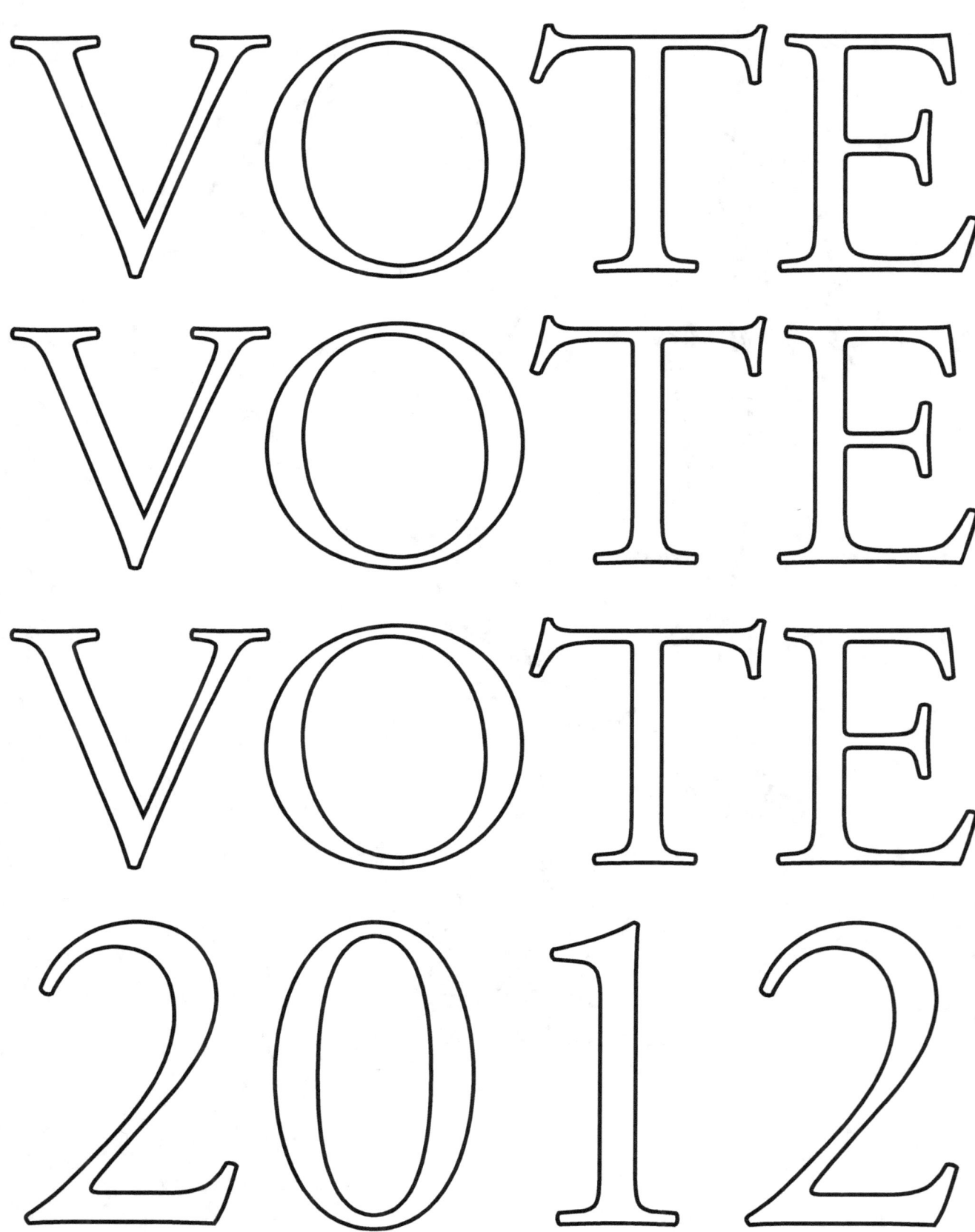

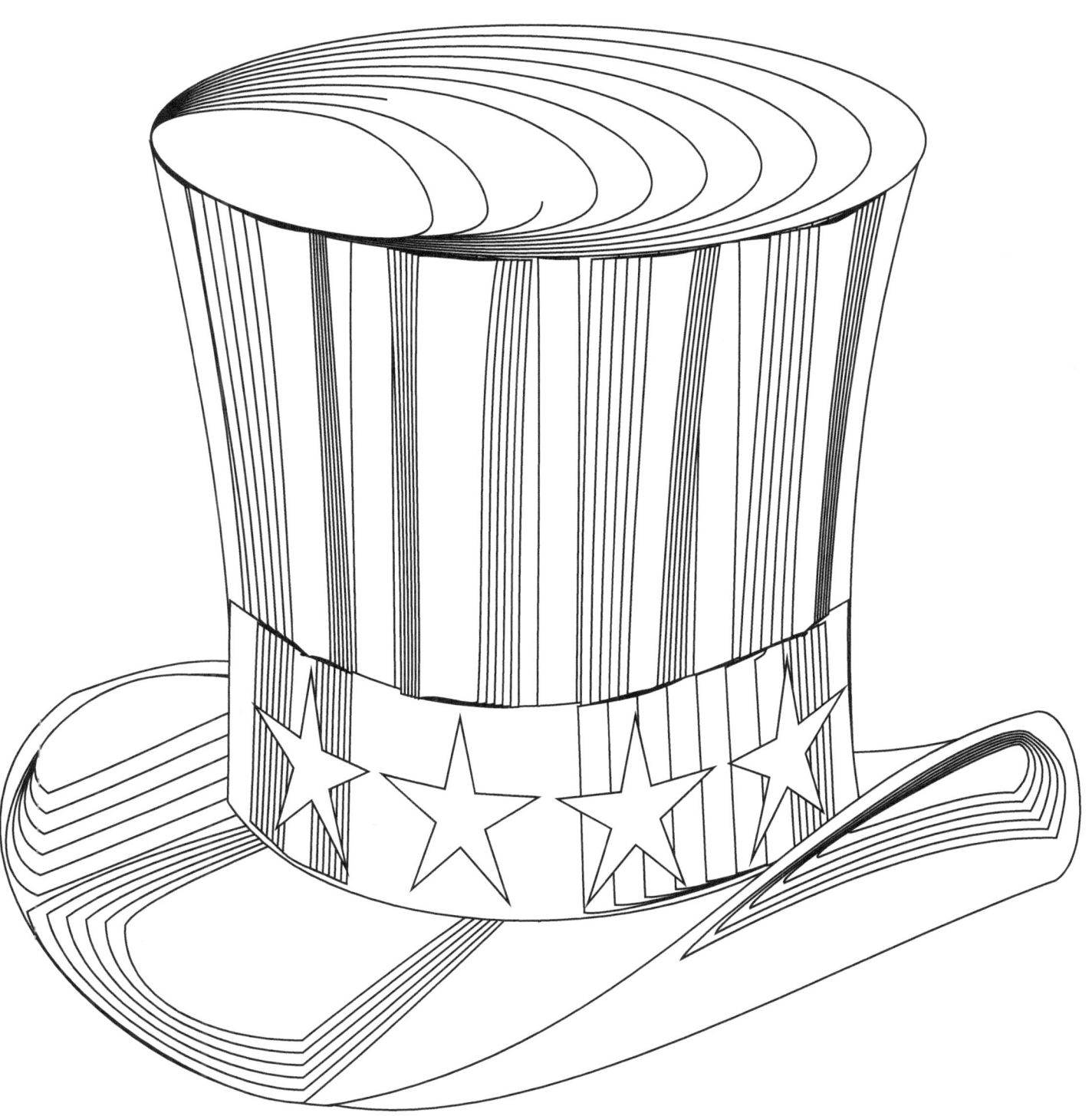

Copy, Color and Play Tic Tac Toe

Major Democratic and Republican Candidates

DEMOCRATIC
President Barack Obama
50-years old

REPUBLICAN
U.S. Representative Michele Bachmann
55-years old

Herman Cain, Businessman
65-years old

Former Speaker of the House Newt Gingrich
67-years old

Former Governor of Utah and Ambassador to China
Jon Huntsman
51-years old

U.S. Representative Ron Paul
75-years old

Governor of Texas Rick Perry
61-years old

Former Governor of Massachusetts Mitt Romney
64-years old

Former U.S. Senator from Pennsylvania Rick Santorum
53-years old